# LUCKY HARES
## AND ITCHY BEARS

and other
### ALASKAN ANIMALS

POEMS BY
## SUSAN EWING
ART BY
## EVON ZERBETZ

*Evon Zerbetz*

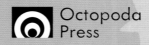

Octopoda Press

# BROWN BEAR

Discovering the tracks of Bear
can give you quite a little scare.

You hope you don't (you hope you do!)
see the bears ahead of you.

If you're careful, if you wish,
you'll find your brown bears catching fish—

Or ((SCRATCHING)) up against a tree,
to itch their bear behinds with glee.

# SEA OTTER

Imagine munching urchins
while floating on your back,
and conking clams upon your chest,
it's WHAM, and then CUH-*RACK!*

For Otter it's not awkward
to snack or snooze afloat,
he bobs upon the ocean waves
just like a furry boat.

And when it's time to sleep,
he rests his whiskered head,
tucked in with friendly fishes
in his seaweed waterbed.

# RAVEN

Listen to that raven as he swoops high over town,
*kawling* to his friends to watch him flip-fly upside down.

*KAH!* Says one,
       that's nothing—want to see me catch a mouse?
Kah *HA!* Another cackles,
       race you out to Fido's house!
Kah-ha-*HA!* They call out back and forth,
       in laughing raven words
(you know, of course, that ravens are the smartest of all birds).

I like to think I've figured out the things that ravens say,
about their shiny treasures and tomorrow's garbage day.

To be a raven flying free would be my dream come true,
I'd stretch my wings and

**whoooosh**

       around and show off just for you.

# SALMON

When you spy a salmon
swimming hard upstream,
she's had more frights and seen more sights
than you could ever dream.

She moved from stream to ocean
when she was just a kid,
she had to outrun orcas,
she dined on squiggly squid.

Now with a school of siblings
all fighting to get home,
she shimmies past a fishing bear
and leaps through falls and foam.

Nose into the current,
she finds the place she knows—
she lays her eggs where she was born,
and on the story goes . . .

# WOLF

Nose licking, tails wagging, paws pawing ears,
it's family reunion when Big Wolf appears.

Now father and mother and pups in a pack
set off in starlight to sniff breeze and track.

They pause for a moment in milky moonlight,
to wonder who else is out hunting tonight.

*HOWWWWIIIIIIOOOOOO* they sing out . . .
                                    then let silence fall,
to listen for neighbors returning the call.

# MOOSE

You know it's not polite to stare—
still, moose can give you pause.

Those skinny legs! Those droopy ears!
How does he blow that schnozz?

But with his legs he's happy,
with his nose content.

Moose can walk forever
and smell the smallest scent.

He can wade in water
above his knobby knees.

But if a leaf gets up his snoot—
Watch out! He's gonna S N E E Z E !

# CARIBOU

Yoo-hoo, Caribou, where are you going now?
Is migration like vacation? Excuse me? Mrs. Cow?

You spend the winter over there, the summer over here,
and have your baby on the way—is travel your career?

Your tiny calf is born to go, it really is quite stunning,
before her birth-day's over she's already off and running.

Your little girl is lucky to be born a caribou,
just like the boys, she gets to grow some spiky antlers, too!

# WALRUS

I wouldn't kiss a walrus any time or any place,
for such a smooch could suck the nose right off my little face

You see, the walrus eating style—which seems to work quite well,
puts tongue and lips to work to vacuum seafood from the shell.

Upside-down, they feel around for food with whiskered muzzle,
nosing clams out of the sand, giving crabs a nuzzle.

They use their tusks for *other* tasks, but let me be quite honest,
if I had teeth like *that* I'd call my brother's orthodontist.

## DRAGONFLY

Mosquito didn't have a chance,
when Dragonfly asked, "Shall we dance?"

She waltzed Mosquito north and south,
he jitterbugged into her mouth.

*"Gotcha!"* grinned sly Dragonfly,
hovering lightly in the sky.

And with a *thrumm* she whirred away,
"Who else would like to dance today?"

# HUMPBACK WHALE

Humpback leaps at any chance
to prove you don't need feet to dance.

He pirouettes from sea to air,
*a-splash* with wild cetacean flair!

His flippers flap like whaley wings,
or like a maestro's motionings.

When—$sp^{oo^oo}sh$—he dives without a trace,
the ocean seems a quiet place.

# FLYING SQUIRREL

Flying Squirrel runs to the tip of a branch
and launches herself into  s p a c e . . .

She sails down a moonbeam,
     slips safely past Owl,
          with easy, unflappable grace.

Gliding from cedar to spruce on
a parachute cape made of soft furry skin,

it's nighttime, the right time,
     to be up and at 'em–
          it's dark out, her day can begin.

Nosing around on the ground, see her skitter . . .
*skip, scamper, scurry and snuffle,*

working to dig up her most luscious treat,
a yummy plump mushroomy truffle!

# EAGLE

Smaller birds weave cups of grass
entwined with spider thread.

But eagles build **humongous** nests
with big old sticks instead.

They need such massive structures
to hold their giant twins,

who hunker in the woodsy crib
like feathered bowling pins.

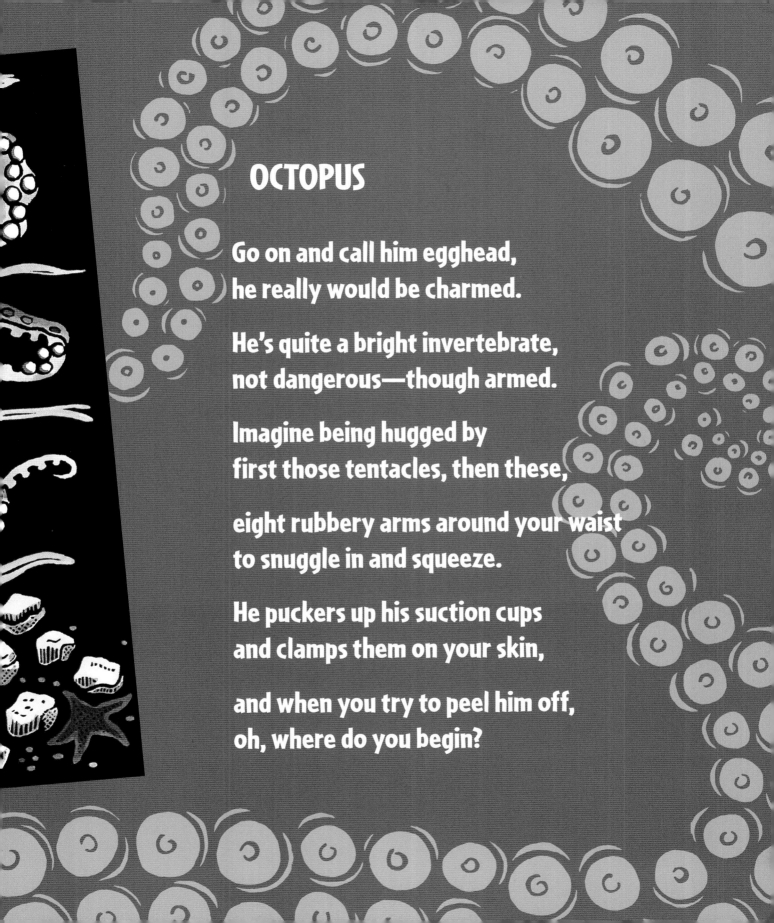

## OCTOPUS

Go on and call him egghead,
he really would be charmed.

He's quite a bright invertebrate,
not dangerous—though armed.

Imagine being hugged by
first those tentacles, then these,

eight rubbery arms around your waist
to snuggle in and squeeze.

He puckers up his suction cups
and clamps them on your skin,

and when you try to peel him off,
oh, where do you begin?

# SNOWSHOE HARE

Oh my gosh, I've got to *r u n*—
Lynx is here to spoil the fun!

My feet are built to tread the snow
but so are hers—that girl can go!

Oh no! She's gaining—
           *a spurt of speed*—
am I to be her bunny feed?!

Zig, zag, dash I'm past her,
Today *my* furry feet are faster!

I never ever want to lose
my lucky little running shoes.

Text © 1996 and 2012 Susan Ewing
Illustrations © 1996 and 2012 by Evon Zerbetz

Originally published by Alaska Northwest Books®, Portland, Oregon, 1996
Second edition published by Octopoda Press, Ketchikan, Alaska, 2012
Second Printing 2016

Library of Congress Control Number: 2012947453

ISBN (SB) 978-0-9858506-1-6

Design: Elizabeth M. Watson, Watson Graphics
Editorial: Marlene Blessing
Digital Prepress: William Campbell, Mars Premedia
Production Coordinator: Susan Dupèrè

The artwork for this book is produced from Evon's hand-painted linocuts. To see more of Evon's linocuts, mixed media, and public art installations visit her portfolio at www.evonzerbetz.com

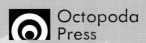 Octopoda Press

P.O. Box 8943
Ketchikan, Alaska 99901
907.225.8212
www.octopodapress.com

Printed in China

# FROG

Froggy Boy, I have to ask ya,
whatcha doin' in Alaska?

How do you survive the chill?
Do you hop south? Down to Brazil?

*No! Snowy blanket tucks me in,
from froggy feet to froggy chin.*

*And so I'm quite content to doze
while all the world around is froze.*

*When spring days come, we groggy frogs
crawl out from under soggy bogs,
waking up from winter's sleep,
Uh-ribbet*

**Croak,**      Reep

Uh-Reep

Reep